This book was purchased
with money from
"BLISTERS FOR BOOKS"

WORLD HABITATS

FORESTS and WOODLANDS

Rose Pipes

RSVP

RAINTREE
STECK-VAUGHN
PUBLISHERS
A Steck-Vaughn Company

Austin, Texas

Published by Raintree Steck-Vaughn Publishers,
an imprint of Steck-Vaughn Company

A ZOË BOOK

Editors: Kath Davies, Pam Wells
Design & Production: Sterling Associates
Map: Sterling Associates
Design Management: Joyce Spicer
Electronic Production: Scott Melcer

Library of Congress Cataloging-in-Publication Data

Pipes, Rose.
      Forests and woodlands / Rose Pipes.
          p.   cm. — (World habitats)
      "A Zoë book"—T.p. verso.
      Includes glossary and index.
      Summary: Introduces some notable forests and woodlands around the world, including the taiga in Russia, the eucalyptus woodlands in Australia, and the mangrove forests of Central and South America.
      ISBN 0-8172-5007-7
      1. Forests and forestry — Juvenile literature.   2. Trees — Juvenile literature.
3. Trees — Utilization — Juvenile literature.   4. Forest ecology — Juvenile
literature.   [1. Forests and forestry.   2. Trees   3. Forest ecology.   4. Ecology.]
I. Title.   II. Series: Pipes, Rose. World habitats.
SD376.P57   1999
333.75'09 — dc21   97-46517
                                                                                          CIP   AC

Printed in Hong Kong by Midas Printing Ltd.
Bound in the United States
1 2 3 4 5 6 7 8 9 LB 02 01 00 99 98

Photographic acknowledgments

The publishers wish to acknowledge, with thanks, the following photographic sources:

Environmental Images / Irene Lengui 22; / Chris Martin 25; The Hutchison Library / Andrey Zvoznikov 14; / Edward Parker 23; / Nick Owen 29; Impact Photos / Jonathan Pile 27; NHPA / David Woodfall - cover inset bl, 5; / John Shaw 13; / Michael Leach 15; / A.N.T. 19, 21; / Andy Rouse 28; South American Pictures / Chris Sharp - title page; Still Pictures / Francois Pierrel - cover inset tr; / Bruno Cavignaux 7; / Clyde H.Smith 9; / Roland Sietre 16; / Mark Edwards 20; / Thomas Raupach 24; / Michel Gunther 26; TRIP / R.Surman - cover background; / P.Rauter 8; / Viesti Associates © Stephen G.Maka 10; / W. Fraser 12; Woodfall Wild Images / David Woodfall 6; / Lisa Husar 11; / M.Biancarelli 17; / Ted Mead 18.

The publishers have made every effort to trace the copyright holders, but if they have inadvertently overlooked any, they will be pleased to make the necessary arrangement at the first opportunity.

Contents

All the words that appear in **bold** are explained in the Glossary on page 30.

Where Do Forests and Woodlands Grow?

Trees need a lot of water. So forests and woodlands grow in places where plenty of rain falls. Many different kinds of trees grow in each type of forest or woodland.

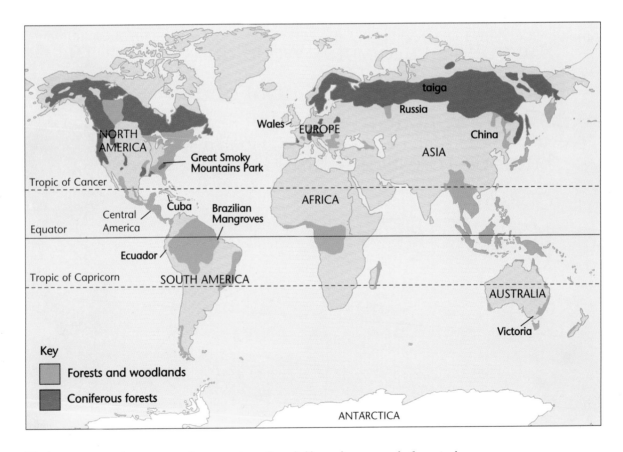

This map shows where to find the largest forests and woodlands around the world.

Coniferous trees can grow in places where winters are long and cold. Most coniferous trees have green, needle-shaped leaves all year. They are **evergreen** trees.

Deciduous trees have flat leaves that change color and drop in the autumn. Deciduous woodlands grow in milder, wetter places than coniferous forests. Some woodlands have both deciduous and coniferous trees.

There are deciduous and coniferous trees in this woodland in Wales.

Wildlife in Forests and Woodlands

Thick, coniferous forests are too dark for flowers to grow.

In open, deciduous woodlands, sunlight can reach the ground below the trees. Wildflowers, like these bluebells, grow there.

Trees provide food as well as homes for birds and other animals. Animals eat the nuts, fruits, leaves, seeds, and bark from trees. Some animals make nests in tree trunks or branches. Most forest animals are **adapted** to living in trees.

This red squirrel has sharp claws to help it to climb. The squirrel also has strong, sharp teeth that can crack open hard nuts.

Using Forest Trees

We use wood to make buildings, furniture, and many other things. Tree nuts, fruits, leaves, oils, and **sap** also have uses. Some can be eaten or used to make medicines.

These trees are cut for their wood, or lumber.

Cutting down trees destroys **habitats**. In many countries there are now special parks and nature **preserves**. Here, the trees and the wildlife are **protected**.

In northern lands, acid rain, a kind of **pollution**, has killed many trees. The rain picks up gases from factory smoke, cars, and trucks. It falls as rain, sleet, or snow. Then, it damages, or harms, the trees when it falls on them. Gases from Pennsylvania can kill trees in Vermont.

These dead trees are in the Blue Ridge Mountains near Asheville, North Carolina. Acid rain killed this spruce and balsam forest.

North America's Mixed Woodlands

Mixed woodlands grow in the central and eastern United States and in southeastern Canada. The trees are mostly deciduous, such as hickories, maples, birches, and oaks. But

These beautiful woodlands are in Maine.

evergreen pines like firs, balsams, hemlocks, and spruces also grow there.

There are towns, roads, and cities in the United States' woodlands. Many woodland animals died out because they lost their habitats or because of hunting. For example, the beaver is in danger because of hunting.

Other animals, such as raccoons, skunks, opossums, and bobcats, survived. They have adapted to town life. Many raccoons now eat garbage and live inside empty buildings.

Before towns were built, raccoons always lived in trees and ate wild foods.

The sugar maple tree produces a sweet sap that people make into sugar and syrup. One large tree can produce about 5 pounds (2 kg) of sugar. The sugar maple is now in danger from acid rain.

Some woodlands are protected in **national parks**. Many different trees, such as oaks, hickories, hemlocks, and pines grow in Great Smoky Mountains National Park. There are

In Quebec, Canada, the sweet sap drips into buckets.

more than 1,000 kinds of plants and small trees and shrubs with beautiful blossoms. The rare yellow lady's slipper, a wildflower, grows here, too.

Wild turkeys and bears live among the trees. Turkeys are large birds that eat nuts, insects, and seeds. Sometimes they might even eat a small frog. When they are frightened, wild turkeys will run for cover or can even fly for very short distances.

You can see flowering dogwood trees in Great Smoky Mountains National Park in the Appalachian Mountains.

Russia's Coniferous Forests

The largest forest in the world grows across northern Russia. It is known as the taiga. Coniferous trees, or trees that have cones,

Winters in the taiga are very long, cold, and snowy.

grow there. Pines and firs are coniferous trees. They can live through the long, very cold winters in the taiga.

The forest is home to many wild animals. One of the largest forest **mammals** is the lynx. The largest bird is the capercaillie.

Capercaillie eat conifer shoots and tree needles. Smaller crossbills eat seeds from the woody cones of the conifers.

Crossbills use their crossed bills to open the cones. Then, they use their long tongues to reach the seeds.

Lumber from taiga trees is made into wood pulp and paper at paper mills. These mills create a great deal of pollution. Russia **exports** a large amount of lumber and paper.

This paper mill is beside Lake Baikal in Russia. The lake is badly **polluted** by chemicals from mills like this one.

Small parts of the taiga are protected in preserves. Outside the preserves, wild animals are in danger from hunting. Sables and ermines are hunted by humans for their valuable furs.

Wildlife habitats are destroyed when land is flooded to make **reservoirs**, and by forest fires and pollution.

Animals, such as sables and this lynx, are in danger from hunting and loss of habitat.

Australia's Eucalyptus Woodlands

Eucalyptus woodlands cover nearly one quarter of the land in Australia. These trees are called gum trees in Australia. They are one of the tallest trees in the world.

This eucalyptus forest is in the state of Victoria, in southern Australia.

The Australian opossum lives in eucalyptus woodlands. There are many kinds of opossum, and some of them are gliders.

Opossums feed on the leaves, buds, and shoots of gum trees. The sugar glider lives in hollows in the tree trunks. The skin between the front and back legs of gliders stretches out to form wings. It drifts from one tree down to another.

When the glider jumps from a tree, it can glide across to another tree more than 330 feet (100 m) away.

The leaves of gum trees contain a strong-scented oil. This oil and the gum in the trees make them burn very easily.

Forest fires often happen in the eucalyptus woodlands. But the trees are well adapted to fire. After a tree is burned, buds below the bark grow very quickly.

People use gum wood in many ways, such as for fuel, for building, and for making fences. The bark is used in the making of leather and paper.

Eucalyptus trees provide habitats for wild animals such as the koala. Honeyeaters are a type of bird found in these tall trees, too.

Koalas eat the leaves of gum trees and make their homes in the branches.

Mangrove Forests of Central and South America

Mangrove trees grow along the coasts of most **tropical** countries. They grow on flat land that ocean or salt water covers when the **tide**

These mangroves are on the coast of Brazil, a country in South America.

comes in. Many kinds of mangrove trees grow in tropical Central and South America. Some are 145 feet (44 m) tall. Others are only three feet (1 m) tall.

Mangroves form a thick tropical forest. They are well adapted to their coastal habitat. Each tree has long roots, called prop roots, to hold it firmly in the mud.

Some kinds of mangroves also have tiny, pencil-thin roots that grow up above the water. These help the trees to take in air.

You can see both kinds of mangrove roots in the photograph.

People who live in the forests use mangrove wood for fuel. In some places, people try to preserve the trees by cutting off branches instead of cutting down whole trees. This helps to protect the forest habitat for the wildlife and for human use, too.

In Cuba, there are crocodile farms in the mangrove forests. Tourists often visit the farms.

In the past, the mangrove forests have not been protected. In fact, these forests have also been cleared to make boating **marinas** that attract tourists.

In some countries, such as Ecuador, people clear mangrove trees away to make shrimp ponds. They catch and sell the shrimp.

You can see that the mangrove trees have been cut down to make space for this shrimp farm in Ecuador.

Bamboo Forests in China

Bamboo is a treelike grass that can grow as tall as 120 feet (37 m). Scientists think bamboo

In the mountains of western China, bamboo grows in thickets, or clumps, in the forests.

was one of the first grasses to grow on Earth.

Bamboo is strong and can bend without breaking. People use it to make platforms and ladders. There are bamboo musical instruments and furniture. Split bamboo is woven into mats and made into chopsticks. There are many ways to use bamboo.

Bamboo structures on buildings in Hong Kong.

China's pandas live in bamboo thickets found in the mountain forests. Bamboo is their main food, but the bamboo forests are in danger.

A sixth finger on their front paws helps pandas to hold the bamboo while they eat it.

People cut down bamboo forests to make farmland. The pandas who used to live there are dying out because their habitat was destroyed.

There are only about 800 pandas left in China. Now they live in forest preserves where they are protected. Scientists around the world have spoken out to save the panda and its habitat.

Farms in the countryside near Dali, where the bamboo forest has been cleared.

Glossary

adapted: If a plant or an animal can find everything it needs to live in a place, we say it has adapted to that place. The animals can find food and shelter, and the plants have enough food in the soil and enough water. Some animals have changed their shape or their color over a long time, so that they can catch food or hide easily. Some plants in dry areas can store water in their stems or roots.

coniferous: Trees that have cones and needle-shaped leaves.

deciduous: Trees that usually have broad leaves that change color and fall off in the autumn.

evergreen: Trees that have green leaves all year long.

exports: Goods that are sold and taken to other countries.

habitat: The natural home of a plant or animal. Examples of habitats are deserts, forests, and wetlands.

mammals: The group of animals whose young feed on their mother's milk.

marinas: Safe areas for boats to dock, often used for repair and service.

national parks: Laws protect these lands and their wildlife from harm. These places usually have beautiful scenery and rare wildlife.

pollute: To poison land, water, or air.

pollution: Something that poisons land, water, or air.

preserves: Areas set aside for wildlife to live in safely.

protected: Kept safe from changes that damage the wildlife or habitat.

reservoirs: Lakes that have been built to store water for people to use.

sap: A liquid, or juice, that flows through the tree and carries water and food.

tides: The rising and falling of the level of the ocean each day.

tropical: Places that are hot and wet all year are called tropical.

Index

DATE DUE
